YOUR KNOWLEDGE HAS VALUE

- We will publish your bachelor's and master's thesis, essays and papers

- Your own eBook and book - sold worldwide in all relevant shops

- Earn money with each sale

Upload your text at www.GRIN.com and publish for free

Bibliographic information published by the German National Library:

The German National Library lists this publication in the National Bibliography; detailed bibliographic data are available on the Internet at http://dnb.dnb.de .

This book is copyright material and must not be copied, reproduced, transferred, distributed, leased, licensed or publicly performed or used in any way except as specifically permitted in writing by the publishers, as allowed under the terms and conditions under which it was purchased or as strictly permitted by applicable copyright law. Any unauthorized distribution or use of this text may be a direct infringement of the author s and publisher s rights and those responsible may be liable in law accordingly.

Imprint:

Copyright © 2018 GRIN Verlag
Print and binding: Books on Demand GmbH, Norderstedt Germany
ISBN: 9783668719903

This book at GRIN:

https://www.grin.com/document/428099

Dr. Marshall Goldberg

Synchronicity, Causality, Complexity, and the Brouwer Fixed-Point Theorem

GRIN Verlag

GRIN - Your knowledge has value

Since its foundation in 1998, GRIN has specialized in publishing academic texts by students, college teachers and other academics as e-book and printed book. The website www.grin.com is an ideal platform for presenting term papers, final papers, scientific essays, dissertations and specialist books.

Visit us on the internet:

http://www.grin.com/

http://www.facebook.com/grincom

http://www.twitter.com/grin_com

Synchronicity, Causality, Complexity, and the Brouwer Fixed-Point Theorem

© 2018
M. Goldberg

Carl Jung [2] defined synchronicity [1] as an **acausal connecting principle**, and a 'meaningful coincidence.' He first introduced the concept in the 1920s. In 1952, he published the paper "Synchronizität als ein Prinzip akausaler Zusammenhänge" (Synchronicity – An Acausal Connecting Principle), which included a monograph by Wolfgang Pauli [3]. Jung theorized that temporally coincident occurrences of 'meaningful' events are acausal, and not bound by the axiom of causality (AOC), the principle that all effects have causes and all causes produce effects.

In his book *Synchronicity* [2] Jung tells the following story of a synchronistic event: 'My example concerns a young woman patient who, in spite of efforts made on both sides proved to be psychologically inaccessible. The difficulty lay in the fact that she always knew better about everything. Her excellent education had provided her with a weapon ideally suited to this purpose, namely a highly polished Cartesian rationalism with an impeccably "geometrical" idea of reality. After several fruitless attempts to sweeten her rationalism with a somewhat more human understanding, I had to confine myself to the hope that something unexpected and irrational would turn up, something that would burst the intellectual retort into which she had sealed herself. Well, I was sitting opposite her one day, with my back to the window, listening to her flow of rhetoric. She had an impressive dream the night before, in which someone had given her a golden scarab — a costly piece of jewelry. While she was still telling me this dream, I heard something behind me gently tapping on the window. I turned round and saw that it was a fairly large flying insect that was knocking against the window-pane from outside in the obvious effort to get into the dark room. This seemed to me very strange. I opened the window immediately and caught the insect in the air as it flew in. It was a scarabaeid beetle, or common rose-chafer (*Cetonia aurata*), whose gold-green colour most nearly resembles that of a golden scarab. I handed the beetle to my patient with the words, "Here is your scarab." This experience punctured the desired hole in her rationalism and broke the ice of her intellectual resistance. The treatment could now be continued with satisfactory results.'

In another example of synchronicity: 'The French writer Émile Deschamps claims in his memoirs that, in 1805, he was treated to some plum pudding by a stranger named Monsieur de Fontgibu. Ten years later, the writer encountered plum pudding on the menu of a Paris restaurant and wanted to order some, but the waiter told him that the last dish had already been served to another customer, who turned out to be de Fontgibu. Many years later, in 1832, Deschamps was at a dinner and once again ordered plum pudding. He recalled the earlier incident and told his friends that only de Fontgibu was missing to make the setting complete – and in the same instant, the now-senile de Fontgibu entered the room, having got the wrong address.

The phrase 'acausally-connected events' refers to the simultaneous or near-simultaneous occurrence of events which appear related in a meaningful way, yet seem to have no causal connection. Synchronicity, a concept first introduced by Carl Jung, holds that events are "meaningful coincidences" if they occur with no discernable causal relationship.

This paper proposes that synchronicity is:

- not acausal, but causal, and a consequence of the axiom of causality (AOC).
- an emergent phenomenon arising from the complex interactions of causal events.
- the result of a deterministic system modeled by a universal cellular automaton.
- bound by the Principle of Computational Irreducibility (PCI).
- a consequence of the Brouwer Fixed-Point Theorem, BFPT [5, 7].

The Axiom of Causality (AOC) implies that all effects have causes, and all causes have effects. Every 'cause-effect' pair or vector arises from an antecedent cause and, in turn, produces an immediately subsequent effect which is also a cause. There are no causes without effects or effects without causes; the system is closed—every vector comes from a vector and goes to a vector. It is proposed that these vectors can interact with one another in very complex ways which can be modeled by a universal cellular automaton such as Wolfram #110 [4]. Moreover, because the system is 'closed' these vectors can be represented as a vector field on the N-1 surface of an N-dimensional closed surface (e.g. a sphere)—the Brouwer Fixed-Point Theorem (BFPT).

In a universal cellular automaton such as Wolfram #110 [4], the Principle of Computational Irreducibility (PCI) teaches that no 'shortcut' equation can tell us the state of the cellular automaton at some future time merely by 'plugging in' a value (T_{FUTURE}). Instead, one must 'run' the cellular automaton to see its future state. The cellular automaton is deterministic, but *a priori* indeterminable. Furthermore, for a given 'state' of the cellular automaton, it is not generally possible to trace the pathway by which that state was reached, even though it was reached deterministically. To do so would violate the PCI.

In the case of synchronicity we have many causes and effects, including all those causes which can produce effects on memory, and dreams. The mind, in turn, is the cause of other effects on the world, including other minds. In other words, simple immediate (direct cause-effect) vectors, AB, CD, EF (instantaneous 'world lines') can interact with one another in the most complex ways. The word 'immediate' means occurring together over a 'short' period of time where Δt, the time magnitude of the vector, is infinitesimally small.

All of these simple immediate cause-effect relationships can be seen as the elements of a 'rule' defining the computations of a universal cellular automaton where these vectors interact in complex ways.

The Principle of Computational Equivalence (PCE) [4] holds that simple rules, such as Wolfram #110, can lead to complex behavior. A multitude of interactions among these vectors as elements in a complex cellular automaton can result in unexpected causal relationships.

However, the Principle of Computational Irreducibility (PCI) [4] does not allow us to determine by what circuitous computational routes a particular state was reached. The causal relationship is cryptic. This seems peculiar because we expect a deterministic system to be transparent, yet universal computational systems can produce results that are deterministic yet *a priori* indeterminable. Consequently, events can be related causally, but we are fundamentally unable to determine that they are.

The Brouwer Fixed-Point Theorem (BFPT) [5, 7] relates to the Axiom of Causality (AOC) because both are related to closed systems. Accordingly, the vectors mentioned above can be seen as a set of vectors parallel to the surface of a sphere (see **Figure 1** below). The BFPT results in a confluence of these vectors at some region in space and time where these vectors form a WHORL. A related theorem, called the Hairy Ball (Hedgehog) Theorem (HBT) [6] states that one cannot comb a hairy ball smooth (see **Figures 2 and 3** below). In terms of vectors, this means that two or more causally-related vectors can appear together in a WHORL such that they might seem to be acausally-connected events.

Every hairy ball has a whorl or cowlick. Vectors 'circling the whorl' will occupy the same region of space $\Delta(X, Y, Z)$ and the same interval of time $\Delta(T)$. The delta sign, Δ, can be smaller or larger depending how far apart the vectors are on the 'spiral galaxy shape' of the whorl—either on the outer edges of the whorl or tighter in towards the center.

Suppose many of these vectors circling the whorl are causally-related, but the Principle of Computational Irreducibility prevents our 'calculating' the complex chain of causality that connects them. Accordingly, the confluence of these vectors may be seen by a conscious mind as acausal synchronistic events.

There is nothing mysterious about synchronicity. 'Synchronicity' is merely a convenient term that arises because the PCI precludes 'calculating' the complex causal chain connecting events that end up in the whorl created by the Brouwer Fixed-Point Theorem. Arcane, 'new age,' and occult interpretations of synchronicity are seen to be superfluous. A particular human brain with certain memories might interpret these events as an example of synchronicity, even though the events are not directly one-to-the-other causally related except in the mind of the agent ('meaningful occurrence') who observes the events.

To others, without the same memories, the circumstance would not be considered meaningful. Synchronicity is observer specific, and only exists if there are conscious minds able to assign meaning to these events. If Jung's patient that day had not had a dream about a golden scarab, then when the beetle rapped at the doctor's window, there would have been no synchronicity of events noted. Similar events involving one or more people over many years depend on the memories of those involved, and would not be considered synchronicity by others who do not have those connecting memories.

Referring to Figure 3 below, vectors on the outer rim of the whorl and in the same space, but separated in time by a large ΔT, might lead one to interpret the events incorrectly not only as synchronistic, but also that one event, such as a dream, had foreseen or anticipated a 'future' event.

On the other hand, vectors on the outer rim of the whorl occurring at the same time, but separated in space might be interpreted as synchronistic events separated by distance. 'Minds,' including memories and dreams, are part of the world, and are both causes and effects. Minds are able to interact with one another immediately or over various periods of time (seconds to millennia) through communication channels such as direct contact, the internet, shared myths, books, and genetically-determined synaptic connections and neural structures.

The vectors can be represented as parallel to and swirling around on the surface of the sphere.

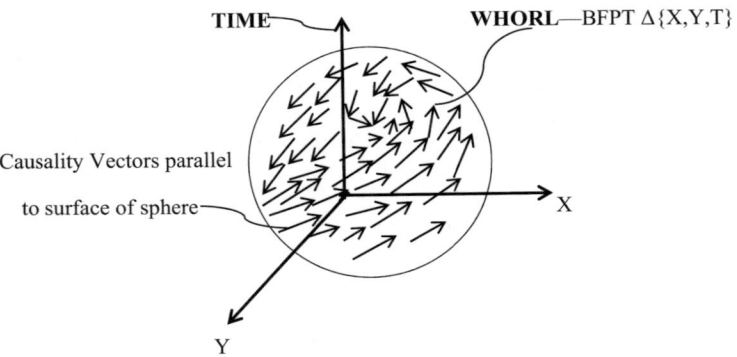

Figure 1 (Authors own work)

Figure 1 above illustrates the Brouwer Fixed-Point Theorem, BFPT [5,6] as a set of short ('direct') cause-effect vectors lying parallel to the surface of a sphere, and forming a whorl or region of confluence. Each vector or element of synchronicity that is part of the whorl may be the result of a causal chain in the past, and could well have occurred at different places, times, and under other circumstances and not have been perceived as an example of synchronicity, but because they are crowded together in the whorl might be interpreted as synchronistic events. The presence of vectors representing 'mind' results in the word 'meaningful.' If the 'ball' in Figure 1 above is oriented to a 3-D coordinate system (X,Y,T), then the whorl represents a region on the ball where the vectors occupy the same region or patch of space and time.

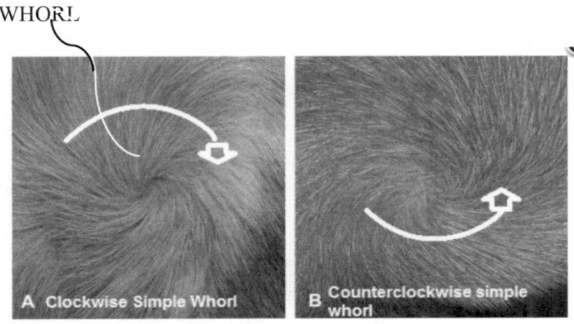

WHORL

A Clockwise Simple Whorl   B Counterclockwise simple whorl

Hair Whorls in the Dog (Canis familiaris), Part II: Asymmetries
Lisa M. Tomkins†,* andPaul D. McGreevy

Figure 2 see reference #10

Figure 2 [10] (after Textbook by Tomkins and McGreevy reference #10) illustrates the Hairy Ball—Hedgehog—Theorem (HBT)—'You can't comb a hairy ball smooth.' Somewhere on the sphere there is a confluence of vectors (hair) forming a whorl. This is an intuitive example of the Brouwer Fixed-Point Theorem. It is proposed, therefore, that Jung's acausal connecting principle or synchronicity actually depends on cause and effect. It arises, paradoxically, from cause and effect. Each causal pair is symbolized as A→B meaning that A is the immediate cause of B, represented as a vector, **AB**. All such vectors taken over a space if that space is convex and closed (e.g., the surface of a sphere), are bound by the Brouwer fixed point theorem (BFPT). Under this condition, there exists a region around which the vectors form a whorl or converge. Although vectors AB and CD within this whorl are connected through a complex and indeterminable network of causation, they can appear to be acausal and, therefore, misinterpreted as an example of synchronicity.

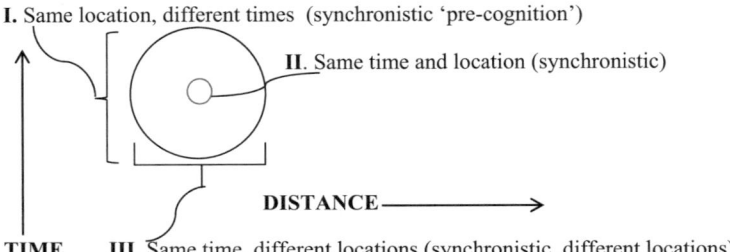

Figure 3 (Authors own work)

Figure 3 above illustrates a representation of a whorl involving vectors AB and CD. Visualize looking directly down at the whorl depicted in Figure 1 above. Time runs vertically, and distance horizontally. Vectors in the same region of space and time may be interpreted as acausally connected (synchronistic). However, this paper proposes that vectors might have been <u>connected causally in the past</u> through a long and <u>non</u>-calculable (PCI) 'chain' of computations of a universal cellular automaton. Synchronistic events for some observers are <u>not</u> synchronistic events for others. Synchronicity depends on events interacting with 'mind'—it is <u>observer-relative</u>. **I.** illustrates the synchronicity of events in the same place but different times, i.e., precognition which may occur if a dream or psychic state and an event are related in the past, but enter the whorl at <u>different times</u> noting that memory has extension in time. **II.** illustrates the usual case of synchronistic events at the <u>same time and place</u>. **III.** illustrates the synchronicity of a psychic state and an event at the <u>same time but in different places</u>. In all these cases, a psychic state and an event have already been causally related in the past, and it is only their relative 'geometric' association in the whorl that determines which case (I, II or III) we assign to the synchronistic event.

'Mind' means all memories and dreams (conscious and unconscious), plus all causes affecting mind, and all effects caused by mind. Causes affecting 'mind' can operate over any communication channel or time interval: person-to-person, electronically, books, myths, other writings, and so forth. Could Jung's archetypes and the 'collective unconscious' refer to those non-specialized, pre-conscious organizations of neural circuitry that are 'hard wired' by DNA? Are there neural structures that have developed through evolution because they confer a selective advantage? Are these structures the syntax that (by computation) becomes the semantic of archetypes? These structures, common to all humans, could mean that unconscious 'patterns of thought' and reactions might exhibit a commonality.

Synchronicity depends on coincidences that have '<u>meaning</u>', implying there must be an agent able to assign meaning. These meaningful coincidences, sometimes over various distances and over many years, seem to arise from the axiom of causality (AOC), and fit with the Brouwer Fixed-Point Theorem (BFPT), and the Cellular Automaton PCI Interpretation of Synchronicity (CAIS). Nevertheless, even without a mind to create 'meaning' there still emerges a whorl-based confluence of vectors in what could still appear despite the absence of 'mind' (at least theoretically) to be an acausal relationship. The Principle of Computational

Irreducibility (PCI) prevents calculation of the complex chain of events connecting causality vectors in the past.

If Gerard 'tHooft [8] and others are correct, the universe can be considered a kind of superdeterministic cellular automaton in which quantum mechanics is a convenient tool for calculations, yet the underlying reality is not probabilistic. Perhaps the notion of synchronicity and its explanation in this paper as a consequence of the axiom of causality is part of a much larger principle involving a superdeterministic universe and counterfactual definiteness. That is, one cannot speak "meaningfully" of the results of measurements that have not been performed, and assume the existence of objects and their properties even if they have not been measured [9].

In conclusion, it is suggested that synchronicity is not acausal, but depends on causality, and is a consequence of the Axiom of Causality (AOC). Synchronicity is observer-relative. The term 'synchronicity' is a shorthand way of saying that while 'meaningful coincidences' do occur and are relevant in understanding our psychic lives, the concept is to be understood as arising from the axiom of causality occurring in a complex, deterministic yet a priori indeterminable system bound by the Principle of Computational Irreducibility, and as a consequence of the Brouwer Fixed-Point Theorem.

References

1. Synchronicity Wikipedia.

2. Jung, C.G. Synchronicity—An Acausal Connecting Principle. From the collected works of C.G. Jung Volume 8. Bollingen series XX. Princeton University Press.

3. Pauli, W. The Influence of Archetypal Ideas on the Scientific Theories of Kepler. Translated by P. Silz In: The Interpretation of Nature and the Psyche. New York and London 1955, Bollingen Series LI.

4. Wolfram, S., *A New Kind of Science* ©2002 Wolfram Media Inc. Wolfram, Stephen, Wolfram Media, Inc., May 14, 2002, ISBN 1-57955-008-8.

5. Brouwer Fixed-Point Theorem. Fixed Point Theorem(s). Wikipedia.

6. Hairy Ball (Hedgehog) Theorem. Wikipedia.

7. Goldberg, M. *On Synchronicity and Causality as Consequences of a Topological Theorem.* Telicom, the Journal of the International Society for Philosophical Enquiry. Vol. XII No. 30. March 1999. ISSN 1087-6456, pp27-34.

8. Gerard 'tHooft. The Cellular Automaton Interpretation of Quantum Mechanics https://arxiv.org/pdf/1405-1548 pdf

9. Counterfactual definiteness. Superdeterminism. Wikipedia.

10. Tomkins, L., McGreevy, Paul D. Hair Whorls in the Dog (*Canis familiaris*), Part II Asymmetries Asymmetries Faculty of Veterinary Science, University of Sydney, New South Wales, Australia First published: 17 February 2010 https://doi.org/10.1002/ar.21077

****

YOUR KNOWLEDGE HAS VALUE

- We will publish your bachelor's and master's thesis, essays and papers

- Your own eBook and book - sold worldwide in all relevant shops

- Earn money with each sale

Upload your text at www.GRIN.com and publish for free